D0222277

The Tragic Type

of

Beautiful

The Journey of Magic and Mayhem

Cheyenne Tyler Jacobs

i

Published 2018

Cover Design by PritiCreative
Edited by Elizabeth Sarah

DEDICATION

This book is dedicated to all of those who have helped me throughout my personal, mental, spiritual, and emotional growth.

As you notice there is no sense of formatting and some poems do not even have punctuation. Well, when you write poetry, it is not structured in a moment of feeling.

It is free and forever changing.

I hope this book shows someone that they are not alone and it is okay to be who you are and say what you think. I hope this book, resonates with the deepest and most sensitive part of your soul. I hope you recognize that at the end of this we are all poetry.

We are all trying to find our way.
Most importantly,
I hope this book gives you the strength to keep pushing.
Even when the world tells you to give up.

Table of Contents

PART I

1

Jealous

Conversations

Painting

Lines

Emotions

Attached

We Wait?

The Truth

Plant

Lies

Did You?

Unlock

Me

Song

Irrelevant

Candy Store

Baby

Moving On…

Depression Is Showing

I Need Answers

For My Bros

Story

School

Slave

PART II

27

Black Girl Depression
Ship
Diagnosis
Over It
Listen
I Don't Feel God
Choices
Minimize
Scar
How?
Graveyard
Parents
Rough Draft
If It's Real
We Should Be Friends
Gorgeous
Anger
All I Hear
Happy Anniversary
That
Darkness
Snapchat
The Lies They Told
She Tastes Like Sadness
I Stopped Looking
What You Did Not Know
I Know You Thought About It
Sober Thoughts
I Should Have Known Better
Thoughts to The Administration
Social Media
His Voice
You Tried
Nothing.

v

(Part II Continued)

I Promise

The Inside

To the Guy I Wish I Could Start Over With

And I Won't Be

Dear, Complacency

Cold

Love

PART III

79

Uprooting

Not Just Your Winter Love

Glass

Black Girl Magic

The Trap

Center

A Woman

Mind, Body, Soul

I Wish, I Wish

My Turn

Tick

Comeback

Do You?

Don't Worry

Cleansing

Can I Rewrite It

With Love

Naked

Priority

(Part III Continued)

Oxygen

Forgive

Poison

Melanin Things

Everything

Possibilities

Ally

Simple

#woke

Appreciation

Bad Things

Gift

Black

Overwhelmed

Path

Fish Bowl

God's Fingerprint

Growth

Victim

You Got a Girl

What is Right?

Torn

Pray About It

Breathe

We Are All Poetry

POETRY

In a sense,
We are all poetry.

We are all
Beautiful,
Tragic,
And Twisted…

Dear, God

I promise to be outspoken

With what has happened to me

I promise to challenge myself

I promise to stand my ground

Amen.

PART I

Jealous

i would say
you hate the person
i am turning into
but lets be honest

since the beginning
you never really understood
who
i was

Conversations

I was waiting for someone to listen.
For someone to allow me to speak my mind,
For someone to allow me to share my heart
I was waiting for a chance.

But I guess some voices go unnoticed.
Which is sad because those very voices,
Are sometimes
The most powerful.

I wish some knew what it felt like to be forgotten.
What it feels like to be set aside,
What it feels like
To feel like you are nothing.

Painting

I always wanted to do makeup.

I loved the idea of it,
The opportunity to change yourself for a moment.
The opportunity to feel like a bad ass in red lipstick!

So red your lips are unapologetically noticeable.
Foundation so strong, no one could shake your confidence.

Concealer so smooth, your weaknesses fade away.
Eyeliner so sharp, it cuts through any doubt you might have.
Mascara so bold, it holds up even your deepest insecurities.

Highlighter so bright, even the light could not match your
shine.
I always wanted to do makeup,
For one night I always wanted to know what it was like to be
beautiful.
Because without it I was just me.

I would be imperfect,
I would be scarred,
I would just be human,

But with a few tubes and brushes,
I could be anyone I wanted to be.
But I can't.
I never learned how to do makeup

Lines

You said we should just be friends,

But I think what you meant,

Was we can be parallel lines.

Forever together,

Just never really crossing.

Emotions

I have memories rolling down my cheeks

slipping out of me like the contents

of a woman's purse on the floor

and I'm scrambling to pick them up

I have so many demons running back and forth in my head

like kids on a playground and still no matter what I do

they won't leave

my secrets are surfacing

And I tried so hard to drown them

in the deepest part of the ocean

but they won't seem to

drown

Attached

i told him i was afraid

he said of feeling good

i told him no

of getting attached

We Wait?

Why do we wait
Until tomorrow?
To move mountains
And create miracles.

When today you woke up
Today God gave you life.
You get another day,
And to be honest

Not everyone was blessed,
Enough to have that.

The Truth

I apologize
On behalf of society
For killing
The younger generation

If only we believed in them
If we only supported their dreams
If only we told them the truth
That they were always Kings and Queens

Plant

we can't plant good things like
Humanity and Change and expect them to grow
if we are standing on poisoned soil
at the end of the day

you can only reap what you sow

Lies

i tried to write about Happy things

but the thing about writing is

you cannot write about what is unfamiliar

so i write about Pain.

that is what i know.

Did You?

i wondered if you looked back
when you left me picking up
the pieces of myself
at the crossroads of

Magic and Mayhem

Unlock

when you kissed me

you unlocked feelings i never knew

you made me feel happiness was reachable

love was believable

that trust was feasible

but then you stopped

you did not look at me the same

you did not want to be with me anymore

and those feelings you unlocked

well.

i am just upset you took the key with you

Me

I killed myself
Yes, I am dead.

Emotionally drained,
Spiritually broken,
Although I am breathing
Does it really matter?

I am not sure when I actually died.
One day I just felt empty,
And yet everyone wanted to keep me breathing
But they do not get it.

It is weird to have to fight your mind.
It feels like someone is whispering in my ear,
Even when I am at a happy point
My mind just does not care.

My mind does not care about me,
And that is weird because it is me
How can I live if I hate me?
If I am destroying me?

That is interesting to think about right?
I realized it recently that I am destroying myself,
That I hate myself
So much.

Song

I hope when you think of me

You think of the good times

Even if we ended on a bad note

Because in my opinion

That note

Should not reflect the full song

Irrelevant

Can we stop that,

that Light Skin vs. Dark Skin thing.

because when we are staring down the barrel of a gun

when they fear us and pull the trigger.

All they see is black.

for them the shade is Irrelevant

Candy Store

I think she wanted it to be him,
But she didn't ask.
Like a child in a candy store,
She selected what was appealing to the eye.

I think she wanted it to be him
The way he laughed at her jokes,
And listened to her stories,
The way he touched her spirit,

She never had someone make her melt.
She pictured herself being free from
Her demons.
Being able to finally say she received love,

Being able to receive what people said
She could never have.
Finally, being able to give
What so many men took from her.
She was happy.
But she left the store
Empty handed,
With another void in her heart.

Like the love she could have received
It vanished and she was left by herself.
She wanted it to be him.
But it wasn't.

And she was still hungry
For what no one could give her.

Baby

You only called me Baby
When you wanted something
I never really noticed it
But today I did

You only called me Love
When I said I was over you
And as many times as I tried
Your number just never seemed to delete

I am also convinced
You even only texted me
When you felt in your heart
I was getting tired of you
You only really kept me
Just in case you needed to use me
I did not see it then
But I realize it now

Once you realized
You could not use me
You left me
You just left me

It is okay though
It did not hurt that bad
If there is one thing I am used to
It is being left

Moving On...

And no matter

How many times

My finger hovered over

Delete

I could not seem

To erase you

From my

Life

Depression is Showing

your Depression is showing
in those late night hours,
while everyone is sleeping
you are awake.

waiting,
for the moment happiness
will overtake you.
but it just hasn't,

your Depression is showing.
and if you miss work again
i am pretty sure they will
fire you this time!

maybe you can fake being sick again?
that worked last time,
maybe you can fake a death in the family?
is there anyone you haven't killed yet?

oh no,
an invite to go out again,
you can't keep missing
these events
...

...
tell them you have to work!
shit. they know you don't work that shift
tell them you are going to church!
then tell God you are sorry for lying.

let him know you'd go to church
but you can't go in this condition.
tell him you'll go next week,
even though that's what you say every week.

your Depression is showing.
and you can't miss another meal,
they notice that stuff
at least eat a piece of bread.

better yet...
make a sandwich in front of them
and take it with you. Boom!
you are a genius.

your Depression is showing.
and with all this energy you are using
trying to pretend to be fine
i hope one day,

you actually Will Be
...

I Need Answers

my heart is heavy

with broken promises

shattered dreams

and hidden thoughts

i do everything

but still feel nothing

For My Bros

I am sorry to the men.
I am sorry that ever since you were boys
You were told
"Act like a man"

Man up
Stand up
I am so sorry
You were taught how not to feel

But here is a secret

I prayed to God
For Superman
I never once
Asked him

For the Man of Steel

Story

And sadly
We teach young girls
That they will be to blame
For the unwanted sexual advances that happen to them

When they choose to be silent
We assure them it must not have been that bad
When they choose to speak up
We punish them for ruining someone else's future

We single these women out
Make them choose between
Victim and Survivor
Before they tell their story

They did not choose
The trauma placed on them
So stop making them choose
How to tell their story

School

we graduate from school

but we cannot graduate from life

we do not seem to always shed the stereotypes

or breakout of the boxes

that others have put us in.

Slave

The money the chains
The diamonds the rings
Busy living for these materialistic pleasures
Some cannot even see the real riches around them

Too busy living in a bubble
Walking the same boring paths others have paved
We are living for this temporary greed
This fleeting fortune hoping to build and save

Well if you're living in bondage to these chains
My friend that means you are a Slave

PART II

Black Girl Depression

Black Girl Depression.
Black Girl Depression.
Yes, I see you…
But, do you see me suffering?

Black Girl Depression.
Is praying to God for strength,
And rolling out of bed at 5:00am hoping to get it together
Black Girl Depression.

It feels like you want to give up
But momma ain't raise no quitter,
And daddy don't want to see no tears,
So against your body breaking.

You get up.

Black Girl Depression.
It is crying in the lower level bathroom at work
Because they didn't raise no baby,
You better wipe your tears and walk in there.

You are a Black Woman and you will always work,
200 times harder.
Just to be treated half as good. Deal with it.
Black Girl Depression.

…

•••

It is wondering when my brothers go out at night,
Will they be the victims of a wrongfully pulled police
weapon?
And a victim of a wrongfully constructed system?
So I have to sit and wonder if they will be wrongfully taken
from me.

Black Girl Depression.

Is knowing the same love I have,
When I wonder about the wrongful sins committed against
Black Men.
Some will wrongfully speak against me,
When they say they do not date Black Girls because we have
too much attitude.

Black Girl Depression,
Is me, wondering when I walk into a room
Is it my color or my gender you see first?
And which one if not both…will you make me surrender?

Black Girl Depression.
Is keeping a smile,
While carrying the dreams of my family, the stereotypes of
society,
And pressure on my mind and back!

•••

•••

And you better not ask for help.

Black Girl Depression.
I wish we spoke about you more,
I wish we wrote more poems about you,
I wish more that we stopped implementing you.

In every young Black Girls brain
From birth,
We make her fight so many battles
Oh Black Girl.

I see you fighting, pushing, and moving mountains.
I see you trying to change the game while rolling the dice
I hope you know your feelings are not forgotten,
Your sadness and stress should never be written off.

Oh Black Girl
I see you,
And I am sorry
Oh Black Girl.

I am sorry,
I am sorry
We have Black Girl Depression.

•••

Ship

I am alone.
Not physically
But mentally and emotionally
I am a single ship in the ocean
Where there seems to be no destination

I have been sailing for awhile
And I still have no sense of direction
Neither any destination
And you punish me for that

As if everyone's destination is clear
As if everyone's journey is the same
As if you could ever understand
What it's like to be on my ship

I am tired.
I am tired of sailing.
And that is okay.
Because the rule of the sea is,

A captain must always go down...with their ship.

Diagnosis

Tired of young girls and boys

Facing social rejection

Because depression and anxiety

Are diagnosed by skin complexion

Over It

I was always told
"get over it"

I tried but I am not sure
How to get over the constant fear
Of digging up my old thoughts
Buried in the unmarked graves in my subconscious

I am afraid
That when someone tells me they can be trusted
They are really just looking
To take down my walls

I am afraid
That I will be labeled
Broken
Because I can't seem to open my heart

I will be labeled a victim
Because I tell my story
I am afraid
That I will have kids one day

...

•••

And they will see
Mommy
Depressed
On the kitchen floor

I can't get over
The thought that one day
My mind might get the best of me
And no one will pick up the phone

So no I can't get over it
And I won't
I instead want to grow from it
I want to heal

And love
Even the ugliest parts of my mind
But I hate to inform you
You just do not get over it

And I won't just get over it.

•••

Listen

You heard me breaking.
I know you heard me
You heard my screams,
The bottles rolling across the floor,

You heard me ask God for a reason.
You heard me dying.
And yet you said nothing,
Only a few steps away

Did you want me to break?
Did you believe it would help me in some way?
Or did you not want to help me anymore?
Because you heard me dying.

Did you resign from being a friend?
Did you resign from caring about me?
Was that your formal resignation?
Was that the moment you officially let me go?

...

...

Because you heard me dying.
Was it my fault?
Because, I wanted you to save me?
Everyone else was out of reach.

But you.
Oh you my friend,
You were there
And did nothing.

You heard me dying
And did nothing.
So I can only assume,
You were waiting for me

To take my last breath.

...

I Don't Feel God

I do not feel God anymore
I do not hear his voice anymore
I did once
A long time ago

I blame people
God wants us to love him
But we as people create prerequisites
To God's love

I feel most churches
Create tests
To deem others worthy of God's love
Because that is exactly what God wants

For us to judge each other
And deem each other worthy
Of being able to praise his name
Yep.

That's exactly what God wants…

Choices

You didn't want to lose him.

but,

i don't think you wanted to lose yourself

either.

Minimize

I do not talk about my feelings
Not because I cannot verbally express myself
But because those around me do not let me
My feelings are too extra for them
They try to minimize my feelings
Because apparently I have no issues
But the pain in my heart
Would say otherwise

They try to minimize my feelings
Because apparently I do not know pain
They minimize my feelings
Because apparently I have nothing to worry about
But I have a voice in my mind
And when I am sad it tells me I should just die

They minimize my feelings
Because apparently I am just dramatic
But I have more pain than you can imagine
I am just not allowed to broadcast it

They minimize my feelings
Because they never asked how I feel
I have always been told to get over it
Maybe that is why I am so angry
They try to minimize my feelings
Now even I do not recognize them.

Scar

I will never forget your room number.
Let's rephrase…
I tried to forget your room but who could forget
The smell of cigarettes and beer?

I keep picturing your strobe light stereo system
And how often you were told to turn the volume down.
Yes, I remember it all.
I remember how much you procrastinated

On your homework
And how much you hated typing papers.
I remember when I was not feeling happy
You would always knock on my door and lift my spirits.

I also remember when your feelings for me started to shift
When you no longer looked at me with love.
When you no longer laughed
At my corny jokes or awkward personality.

When you no longer wanted to hold my hand
As we walked to class together.
I remember when we stopped walking to class together.
I remember the first time you yelled at me

Because I did not want to kiss you in public.
You were so mad
Like really mad.
So I learned how to be okay showing affection.

...

•••

But you did not notice that my kisses were cold,
But I guess you did not care,
And I did not care
That you did not care.

I want you to know though I hated kissing,
I am not sure if it was a physical dislike
Or if spiritually I felt I should not be sharing a connection
With you just yet.

I just knew kissing did not feel good to me,
It felt weird.
Then one day you wanted more than kisses,
They did not fulfill you anymore.

And I could not give you more
And that sadly,
Is where our story
Comes to an end.

•••

How?

You were supposed to be better than this
You were supposed to move mountains
And you were supposed to
Make waves that would make the

Ocean look in wonder

See from Birth
You were supposed to make all the suffering worth it
To make up for the losses of those that came before you
You have been fighting battles you did not even know about

And you were supposed to win

Graveyard

And in the end she just killed herself
Not literally but figuratively
She died in her 20s and the jewelry she wears
Doesn't match how expensive
Her mental graveyard is worth

Untapped potential
Unnoticed skill.
Dead Dreams
…they killed her.

Not on purpose of course
To the naked eye
You might even say they tried to help
But the thoughts of needing help scared her
She would have suffered.
Her pain and esteem
Killed everyone else's joy.
They walked on eggshells with her

They didn't know how to talk to her
Some were afraid of her
She had too many people in her head
Even she couldn't tell you who was speaking

So.
Mentally, she killed herself
And the saddest part?
You probably didn't notice it.

Parents

forgive your parents

they tried their best

they were trying to give you Heaven

while fighting their own demons in Hell

Rough Draft

I am tired of editing my story
So those reading it are "comfortable"
My apologies but sadly
My story was not meant to be

"comfortable"

It was meant to speak truth
It was meant to give hope
It was meant to show someone out there
They were never alone

Why must I chew my words
So they are "comfortable" to those listening
My love
When was pain ever "comfortable"?

You cannot love me

And when I say
You cannot love me
I mean you cannot love me
When it is easy

...

...

You cannot love me
Only when I am
Smiling
That is easy

Anyone can do that
I need you to love me
When my world is crashing
At 3:00am
And hope starts slipping

I need you to love me in those moments
I need you to love me in those hours
If you still choose to love me at all
Please...don't just love me when I am whole

Don't just love me
When it is comfortable
Love me

While I am a rough draft

...

If It's Real

if you want to know if it is real

see how your number is saved

if it is saved at all

We Should Be Friends

"I decided we should be friends,"
Of course you would make that decision

After you took what was never yours.
What did you come here for?
If not my heart sir, then what?
If it was merely my body, just say that.

Why allow me to believe you thought more of me?
Why allow me to think someone could love me,
Like the storybooks I once read as a child?
Why allow me to believe…love could exist?

Beyond the hidden pages on dusty shelves.

I guess this is why they do not trust my opinion.
I try to see the shining light in monsters.
I give them a chance and ignore the poison on their lips.
I ignore the scratches on my heart and excuse them often.

•••

...

But I have learned the secrets of monsters.
They count on kind souls ignoring their true form.
They allow themselves to step out of the darkness of a
Closet, from under the deep depths of a rigid bed.

And they decide to instead hide in your bed sheets.
In your soul.
They decide to wrap themselves up in your mind,
Knowing that even when the light comes...

They will never truly disappear.
I wish they would have taught me that.
That even in the light.
Monsters still exist.

...

Gorgeous

i am that "if she was" pretty.
it is different from how my friends are pretty,
or how other girls are pretty
it is a, you "could have been" pretty.

you know that "if she was pretty"
if she was shorter she would be pretty,
if she was not always talking she would be pretty,
if she was not always sad she would be pretty.

if she was not her,
i think she would be
drop dead
Gorgeous.

Anger

I am not angry

Actually I am pissed off

I am furious

The high levels of passion in my heart

Mixed with rage

Is rushing through my bloodstream

It has boiled over

And I am so done

With my passion

Being twisted

Into anger

All I Hear

Here we go again
When I am doing good
It is really good
But when I am doing bad

It feels like my mind is melting
I am afraid you will call me a head-case
Again.
For the 50,000th time

I am not a head-case.

But the more you say it
The more I am starting to believe it
I am starting to believe
All of it

I wish you knew how hard I try
How hard I fight my own thoughts
How hard I try to think "positive"
How hard I try not to hear you

But that is all I ever hear
In these moments
No matter how hard I try
All I hear is you

Happy Anniversary

I think the worst anniversaries are the ones

That remind, us of pain.

Those are the anniversaries you wish

You could erase from your mind.

But they seem to always be circled on your calendar.

And as I sit and remember the day I felt my life

No longer become mine.

I remember the date that will always stay

Stuck in my mind.

I remember the choices that will

Always be in my heart.

I remember it all

And it will always be on repeat.

Happy Anniversary to Me.

That

Why do we teach our girls "that"?
You know "that"…the "that" we tell them.
"That" their strength is in
How many beatings they can endure.
And their beauty is as strong as the matching concealer
They use to hide their pain.

We teach them to be a "good woman" you must accept being
Mistreated,
Misunderstood,
And Misrepresented

Just to get the title Mrs.

What good is that?
What good is Mrs. if you only sit in silence?
You sit missing the days when you use to speak up.
If you can even remember those days.
As a woman I am not sure the exact age
But somewhere we start to shift.
We believe that a boy hitting us on the playground,
means he loves us so much.
That we extend the playground to the dining room table and
bathroom floor.

If you get hit there, it just means he loves you more right?
Apparently, the more pain you have to hide
the more your love is real.

Darkness

he loved me for my black skin

but he never broadcasted that love for me

i guess our love could not be shown in the light

i guess he really had a thing for the dark

considering, that is where he kept me.

Snapchat

You had my Snapchat
It was Friday
July 14, 2017 and your name
It was the first one to pop up

Your Snapchat story.
I could not hide my curiosity
So I watched
You were with your family and friends

You looked so harmless

The sun hit your face and your mom kissed your cheeks
Maybe if she kissed your lips she would taste the poison
Do your friends know how you lie and take from girls?
Or do they just not care?

...

...

How I wonder if they know the souls you have snatched
If they know the happiness you have stolen
Or if they think you are just a good athlete
But, you are not even that good truth be told

You had my Snapchat
And I wondered how that slipped through the cracks
I thought I blocked your existence
But I did not and you still show life on my phone

And you are still living happily.
That is my fault I should have put you on blast
But I couldn't
Deep down somewhere
I guess I still wanted you

He had my Snapchat
And I wonder how many times he has viewed my life
But I wonder even more
How many think his life is amazing?

...

The Lies They Told

Why are we crying at a country

That seems to be ripping at its seams

That was stitched together

On lies anyway

People are mad at a system

They put their faith in

A system they put their trust

I mean have you seen this

World lately

Was it really

Supposed to protect

Any of us

She Tastes Like Sadness

her lips
tasted like
Liquor and Lies
the liquor
she used
to drown her problems
into her subconscious
the lies
she tells
to assure others
she is okay
if you really focus
i am sure
you can
taste both

I Stopped Looking

I am still finding myself
And I think the biggest question I have
Is when exactly
Did I lose myself?

What You Did Not Know

You said you wanted me
But you didn't really
Or rather you couldn't want me
You don't even know me

You know my resume
My Instagram smiles
You know my highlight reel
But you don't know the deleted scenes

You don't know that I laugh loud
To silence the depressing thoughts in my head
You don't know how I FaceTime the same 3 people at night
Because they're the only ones who make me smile

You don't know that I talk to people
Because the voices in my head are always in my ear
Do you know I cry every night
When my mind is quiet

...

...

Because the thought of sitting with myself
Truly and deeply hurts me
I hate myself more than you can imagine
And that's why your "I like you" means nothing

But you wouldn't know that
You don't know me
You didn't want me
Sweetheart like everyone else

You wanted my representative.
The fake me, the box me
The cut me, the edited me.
The good girl and superwoman me

Well that's not me…it never was…and never will be again.

...

I Know You Thought About It

Doesn't matter

How much sleep I get

When my mind and spirit are exhausted

That's a different tired

That's the type of tired

That sleep doesn't cure

It is the type of tired

That only that

Special something

Can cure

Sober Thoughts

some of us

are so good

at finding

happiness

at the bottom

of a liquor bottle

or at the end

of whatever

we are smoking

we are so good

we forget

how to smile

when

sober

I Should Have Known Better

I loved you even when
There was nothing really to love
I saw your potential
But maybe if I saw your reality

I would not have wasted my time

Thoughts to The Administration

Trying to sell our nation this dream
That you want to make this country
Great again
Tying to once again convince

Us we were always equals
But you're the same ones
Who cross the street
When you see black people

Social Media

I am pissed about social media
We ruin relationships because of likes
Couples stay ready to fight
So what you are saying is

You are going to let:

Hashtags,
Comments,
DM's,
Followers,

And underscores
Undermine your relationships?
Sweetheart just because
You have the password to their phone
Doesn't mean you'll ever get the combination to their loyalty

It won't get you the key to their soul
It won't get you the answers to your questions
So stop asking all these people
FOR THEIR DAMN PASSWORD

His Voice

I do not feel God anymore

I do not hear his voice anymore

I did once

a long time ago

when I was younger

and more innocent

before the world got to me

I once heard his voice

You Tried

To the boy who tried to sleep with me
Congrats you unknowingly signed up,
For an emotional breakdown you probably did not want.
Mixed with tears and anger,
I'll tell you that I trust you, and I am fine.
Then about 10 minutes in,
You'll touch me and I won't be able to handle it.

Memories will start pouring into my brain.
And I will express them through my tears,
It will look like I am crying...because I am.
You'll get all freaked out,

OMG she is crying female tears.
What did I do?
Nothing, you did what you were supposed to.
You just did not know how broken
The pieces of my heart and mind are, I hide them so well.
So going back.
You'll freak out. I'll cry.
We will both stare at each other,
I'll leave, and delete your number,
Because, why would you call me back?

And you won't call back.
You will never know why I cried in the first place,
As a matter of fact, no one ever knew why I would cry.
No one has ever called back.

Nothing.

when you touched me
i waited for butterflies and fireworks
to feel completely safe but alive

when you touched me i expected to feel
but i didn't
i still felt cold
like ice, i felt nothing

that's all i seem to feel these days,
Nothing.

I Promise

living in a culture
where catching feelings is bad
is upsetting
when someone
is afraid
of someone dropping
their heart
i promise
it is okay
i promise
i am different
i don't drop
those type of things

The Inside

I smile a little more now
I learned to find happiness
In the small things
I've learned to find it
In the smallest parts
Of myself
I've learned to work
From the inside out
To not look for acceptance
And happiness
I learned to accept myself
And
I became my happiness

To the Guy I Wish I Could Start Over With

She stared at him
Tears rushing down her face
She couldn't help but notice the confusion
In his eyes
And the worry in his mind

She hung on to every word
And slowly she realized
That he would be like everyone else
His words so soothing and nice
Like the words so many others whispered to her

She feared this day
The day she would love him more
Than he could ever love her
He was her bridge when the rain fell

For a moment he made everything calm
For a moment he made her feel safe
For a moment he gave her hope

But then like the beautiful day
Before the storm
She realized that it would
Soon come to end
Because no one could truly
Be a bridge forever

...

•••

She hoped though maybe he would pretend
That they could pretend to be something
She was tired of everyone in her life
Being a memory.

She just wanted someone to be reality
She thought all of this and yet said nothing
Because she already knew the answers
To all her thoughts

He looked at her and smiled
Not even knowing all the things
She had in her mind
He just smiled

His head lowered
And he asked for a second chance
He wanted to start over
He didn't want to hurt her

Let's just start over….hi.

Hi.

•••

And I Won't Be

sadly

sex sells

and i'm

not on the market

Dear, Complacency

I am sorry but I am breaking up with you.
Yes, it is over,
I am through
And I want back all my things.
The dreams and wishes
You said would never come true.
And you can take back your stuff
I do not want it anymore.
The fear,
The doubt,
Nights questioning my purpose
Crying on the bathroom floor.
Complacency, I am breaking up with you
I guess I felt safe with you.
You did not push me to do better,
You just let me sit in my sorrow.
You let me pass by opportunities,
You let me put things off until tomorrow.
Complacency,
It is over.
I hope the next person who meets you
Realizes how toxic you can be.
I mean…there is nothing really left to say
But,
You are no longer good for me.

Cold

I wish you knew what it felt like.
To not be able to express your love,
To be physically closed off,
Even your thoughts can't touch your emotions.

Even your mind can't penetrate your heart,
And even your imagination can't toy with your feelings.
I wish you knew what it was like,
To try and be open and only feel pain.

To look into the eyes of someone you trust,
And watch it turn to someone you hate.
Your mind starts wandering and it goes too far,
The garden of happiness starts to turn into sadness.

The flowers in your mind start to die
And no matter how much you try to cover it up
They see it in your face,
They feel it in your body,

And your pain becomes the elephant in the room.
And you fall cold, so cold.
Soon you will be so cold
You might feel like ice.

Love

However,

I do believe in this thing called Love
Even though it has seemed to
Slip through my fingers
I believe love can heal all
It's the misuse of love that hurts
But love
Real love
That can cure all
If you don't think you have it
It's probably because
You're preoccupied
Trying to look for it
In the same place you think you lost it
Try something new
Look into yourself
You are rooted in love
You see it was always in you
You were always love

PART III

Uprooting

I tried rooting myself into many things
My education,
My job,
My relationships.

But then I realized all these things are seasonal
These things change and we become uprooted
We become displaced
By stuff that should not have kept us grounded

I do not bother now to root myself
In the things that change as easily as the wind
Instead I choose to root myself in my faith
At the end of the day it is the only thing I have

Not Just Your Winter Love

he felt so nice
snuggled next to me
while the snow fell
but it would not work out

i needed someone
to love me
when the weather
was

Warm

Glass

We either look at life
As the glass half empty
Or the glass half full
Such a shame

That our measurements
Could be so black and white
When determining
Our life

When was the last time
You gave thanks
For having the cup
In the first place

When was the
Last time you smiled
Because at any given point
The only thing needed to change your life

Is perspective

Black Girl Magic

I use to ask God
Why I was a Black Girl
Because the world hated me
And I could not grasp why
Then I realized
By the Grace of God himself
We birthed the world
Black is the foundation of everything
That is why they hate us
Because at the end of the day
There is no Them
Without Us
And when you think about it
That is truly Magical

The Trap

I pray you love yourself

The way I do

I hope you will stay authentic

I hope the world doesn't get to you

Center

A wise woman
Once told me
There are really only
Two emotions

Love and Sadness

For everything else
Stems from the two
Happiness, Anger, Jealousy, Fear
It all comes from

Love and Sadness

And if we want to get deeper
We get Sad because of the lack
Of Love
So really

Love is at the center of it all

A Woman

To be a Woman
Is to be a Creator
It is to have a Spirit
And a Soul

To be a Woman
Is to be

Love, Strength, Intelligence
Beauty, Heart, and Creativity
To be a Woman
Is to just be Life

To be
A Woman
Is to be
Just that

It is to Be

Mind, Body, Soul

I'm not sure if I am just overwhelmed
Or over analyzing

But it feels like I am not wanted
For what I have
But more, what I can give
And I can't keep giving myself anymore

I cannot keep giving myself
To those so eager to get physically
Vulnerable with me
But slow to open up their,

Mind,
Body,
And Soul.

What are you afraid of?
That someone might know you
The real you,
And not just the mask you wear.

Show me who you are
It is okay
I promise
I do not judge

I Wish, I Wish

Stop placing your hopes and dreams on me

It is enough to carry what I have

I cannot carry your things and mine too

I am sorry you dropped your dreams when you fell

But, I cannot keep being your wishing well

My Turn

You tried and that is all I can ask
You stayed up and spoke to me
You helped me when I had to cry
You took the glass out of my skin

You tried

You really tried
You deleted numbers
You missed appointments
You tried to peel the devil off my back

You tried to help me breathe
But sweetheart you can't be my life support
We try to keep so many people bright
Who are already dark inside

Life is funny in that way
The people with the biggest smiles
Have the heaviest burdens
Most will never understand

You tried to lift my burdens
But some things are just too heavy
You tried,
And I thank you for that

But,
It is my time to try now

Tick

Even a broken clock
Although not ticking
Its numbers hang
Illustrating the infinite possibilities of

Timing

Comeback

I see them

And they took a step back

But what they didn't realize

Is that they didn't destroy a little girl

They hurt a warrior

So they will always live with fear of attack

They don't know that they hurt an artist

So they'll always live in my work

And they didn't know

When they thought they silenced me

I would

Only come back yelling

Do You?

but do you still think
you are pretty
even when
you don't get likes on

Instagram

Don't Worry

I'll always be with you
You know that moment
When the sun and moon kiss
And the stars align
And your heart starts to
Believe in the possibility of forever
That is where I will always be kept
My love
That is where you can find me

Cleansing

I was never really allowed to cry
No matter where I turned
It was seen as a weakness
But somehow those tears turned to anger

And when I looked into the mirror
I couldn't even recognize myself
So I cry now
I would rather be judged for crying

At least that means I can still recognize myself

Can I Rewrite It

I do not hate anymore
I instead pray for those
Who have persecuted me
And I apologize to those
I have persecuted
We are all on a journey
In this thing called life
We are all writing
Our life story
And I am sorry if you feel
I am a villain
In yours

With Love

Thank you to the

anonymous prayers

that have been sent

to God with love

i might not know

who you all are

but your prayers

are the reason

i am still here today

Naked

I love 2:00am conversations
I want to see you off your game
Not in a negative way
But in the let us get uncomfortable

In an honest way

Let's tell each other about our day
But not in the
"Oh it was cool I had work"
But the

"I am not sure about my purpose,
But I am sure that 5 shots of liquor cures all"

I want to see your mind
In its rawest form
I want us to be naked
Intellectually, emotionally, and spiritually

...

•••

You don't have to take your clothes off
For us to be naked and vulnerable
Take your walls down instead
I can promise that is much deeper

Hang up your pride
And instead put your insecurities on the table
Leave your mask at home
And let us just swim in each other's souls instead

I want to know the secrets
That your parents will never hear
And the secrets
You don't want to tell yourself

Let us dive into each other's
Subconscious
Let us be naked
With our clothes on

•••

Priority

call me crazy
call me stupid
but do not call me
when it is convenient for you

i am not
part-time
downtime
or sometime

you do not get to treat me
like a second option
when i know
that i am a priority

i am a priority
maybe not to you
but to someone i am
and more importantly i am a priority

to myself

OXYGEN

You convinced me my life was meaningless

But you needed me to breathe

We can choose to be many things in life

And today

I stopped being your Oxygen

Forgive

I stopped blaming myself
for what has happened
because i had to realize
it was not my fault
if i could give any advice
it would be to forgive yourself
forgive yourself
while you have the chance

before the world tells you
that you fucked up
before your parents
tell you to be quiet

before your friends
stop answering your calls
and before you
push your emotions so far down
you forget you even had them
please forgive yourself
you deserve it
you deserve

to live life
to live it happily
to live it beautifully
you deserve to live

so go do it.

Poison

i wanted to trust you

but your lips tasted like poison

and i stopped drinking that years ago

Melanin Things

When you are blessed

With Gods given makeup

Of Melanin Magic

The world does seem a little sweeter

Everything

i still have a deep love,
for someone.
who i do not think
will ever love me back.

i am not sure if it is beautiful
that my love goes so deep,
or if it is tragic.
that i cannot move on,

maybe it's beautifully, tragic
like everything else in life.

Possibilities

Maybe in a different life
Where you are more caring
And I was more tough
Maybe we could have been something

But right now, I guess all we can be
Is a bunch of…Maybes
Maybes and
Possibilities
Could've
And should've

In a different life
We could have
And should have
Been together
But I couldn't
Light up your sky
The way you
Painted my soul

So, I guess
I have to accept
That is all we
Will ever be
A bunch of
Could
And Should've
Maybe and Possibilities

Ally

To be a good ally

Is to stand for a cause

Even when

You are not impacted

To be a great ally

Is recognizing

That all of us

Will eventually be

Impacted

Simple

Don't call me Pretty
Pretty is basic
Pretty is boring
Pretty is forgettable

Call me ART
That is powerful
Call me INTRIGUING
That is thought provoking

Call me DIFFERENT
But don't ever call me pretty
Don't ever DILUTE me
To such a MEDICORE level of BEAUTY

Pretty is nice
But I am NOT NICE
I am not AVERAGE
I am not PERDICTABLE

I am many things
And now I finally understand
Why I could never be
Something as SIMPLE

As PRETTY

#woke

I think being woke
Went from being a call
To education and reform
To simply becoming

A really cool hashtag on social media

Being woke is hard
And implementing your knowledge
That is even harder
Listen, it is hard being woke

There are many days
I've wished I could
Turn a blind eye
To the injustices around me

But I cannot
That's the hardest thing
About being woke
You cannot turn a blind eye

Appreciation

You don't appreciate me
You don't appreciate the moments I laugh
You only remind me
Of the nights I constantly cry

As if I do not already know

You don't need my smile anymore
My conversations
My advice
You will only have my memories from now on

Maybe I can make someone else smile
Maybe someone else will enjoy my conversation
But on this day, I am tired
Of trying to perform for people

I can't do it anymore
I have no more walls to break
I have no more tears to give
I have no more time to waste

You don't deserve my smile
So I hope you saved a picture

Bad Things

i do not believe

in the phrase or idea of

"bad people"

even after all the pain

and damage

i believe we are good people

who just do "bad things"

i believe some forgot who they were

before they were swallowed by darkness

so even the light doesn't make sense

i think we need to work harder

to save each other

...

...

we owe it to the world to just try

we need to try

why do we watch people self-destruct

instead of disconnecting the cords supplying trauma

we would rather watch someone be hit by a train

when really we should be yelling

"hey get out the way"

we need to be proactive not reactive

when it comes to saving lives

we need to act

we are not "bad people"

we just do bad things

...

Gift

I get asked often
Why are you tall?
After much thinking
I have an answer

I am tall because
God does not give his gifts out to everyone
He knows
Not everyone can handle such power

I am tall because
When God made me
He needed me to take command
Over whatever room I walk into

I am tall because when God made me
He knew I needed to be gazed upon
For I was always
A masterpiece

I was taught early on to walk into a room
With purpose
I speak with conviction in my voice
I consider myself to be a powerhouse

I am a POWERHOUSE
I mean I am standing
At 6'2
I have no choice

But to be a Powerhouse

Black

Who Am I?
I am Gods love
I am the richest gem in the world
I am all the colors of the rainbow mixed together

I am Black
Unapologetically
And not only in
February

Overwhelmed

My dad told me

You cannot keep using

The word

Overwhelmed

You should not be overwhelmed

If God is the head of your life

And he is in your spirit

You should never be overwhelmed

You are breathing

You are moving

You are capable

So you should never be overwhelmed

Path

i want to love you
but i need to love myself first
don't consider this goodbye
just pray that

our paths cross again

Fish Bowl

i wonder sometimes if some fish know
they are only swimming in a tank or bowl
that they are swimming with barriers
that they are swimming with illusions
fake grass
fake rocks
fake seashells
i wonder if they know
if they swim back and forth
waiting to break free
or if they are completely oblivious
to the fact they are being held in captivity
or were they born into this
never knowing what true freedom taste like
i'd say i hate to be a fish
but i think we all have been guilty

of swimming aimlessly in a bowl.

God's Fingerprint

And when God made you
He made his fingerprint
So even your flaws are beautifully made
And heaven sent

You see why do we care so much
About others expectations?
Why do we care about the societal standards around us?
When we are in the world
But not of the world?

We try so hard to live for the worlds bells and whistles
Trying to take back what was ours from this world.
To be the hero that our ancestors passed down in stories
Because we were the ones they prophesied

But you can't find these heavenly things
With Satan being your tour guide

You are God's fingerprint, his child
And God has favor over you.

But you need to know that first.
Because God's love for you
It goes beyond the walls of the church
It goes beyond the bells and whistles

Growth

God loves me so much

He planted me

To make sure I experience the dirt, ground, and rocks

Because the dirt although messy,

Is a beautiful place

Needed to grow strong people

Victim

I can't be your victim anymore
I'm tired
My tears have run out
My throat is sore from screams
My body aches
From carrying the weight of pain
Around for far too long
I can't be your victim anymore
You do not own me.
You will no longer dictate
The way my tears fall.
I have put up with this for far too long
I am stronger than this
I am bigger than this
I am worth more than this
I am power
I am strength
The drive in my spirit
And the twinkling in my heart
Is worth far more than you ever were
We can all choose to be many things in life
And I choose to not be your victim anymore

You Got a Girl

You said you weren't ready for a relationship
But what you meant to say was
You weren't willing to
Date the girl whose crazy

You weren't ready to commit to someone
Who has to be picked up off the floor
Every few months
I was not good enough for you to love me

You weren't ready for a relationship
But this girl you seem to have a lot of time for
You seem to put the moon and stars in her sky
I wish you could have loved me enough
You told me you weren't ready for a relationship
But you were just a liar
And I was stupid
For thinking you would see something in me

You said you weren't ready for a relationship
But what you really weren't ready for is someone
As powerful and magnificent as me
And that will always be your loss

You said you weren't ready for a relationship
But really…you just could not see, MY worth
And one day you
Will regret it.

What is Right?

I heard when you look in the mirror too long
You are looking for what is wrong.
Even though what is right
Is staring at you in the face

I often wonder when we stare too hard at relationships
Are we looking for what is wrong?
Even though what is right
Is staring right at us?

Torn

If you are looking back at your past
Then you are not looking toward your future
But how do you look at your present?
That's always what I wondered

I do not think you look at your present
I think that is something you feel.
Somehow though we become caught between
Past, Present, and Future

Somewhere we got caught between
Who we were,
Who we are,
And who we want to be.

Somewhere we let
The negative experiences of our past
Make us doubt our future
Now we are stagnant in our present

...

...

Somehow we let
The uncertainty of our future
Make us reside in our past
And we do not think about the present

Somewhere we let
The present slip away
Because the past and future
Are just too close to us

Time.
Time is so interesting
It seems so infinite
And yet so short all at once.

I mean it's crazy to think!
Right this second is your present.
But the moment you started this poem
Is now in the past.

Hope it helps your future.

...

Pray About It

They asked me if I prayed about it
I said I tried to speak to a friend
They asked me if I prayed about it
I said I tried to take a nap

They asked me if I prayed about it
I said I tried to drown it in liquor

They asked me if I prayed about it
I said I tried to eat some dessert
They asked me if I prayed about it
I said I tried to talk to a new guy

They asked me if I prayed about it
I said I tried helping someone else

They asked me if I prayed about it
I said I tried not to think about it
They asked me if I prayed about it
I said I tried to hold back emotions

They asked me if I prayed about it
I said I asked God

They asked me what he said
I said,
He told me to Pray about it

Breathe

Breathe child.
While you can.
And I mean really breathe.
Life is beautiful.
Take the long way home
Stay out a little later than you normally do.
Stay hydrated
And make sure you feel the sand between your toes
Make sure you tell those you love
You love them
While you can
And those bridges you burned
No. you cannot walk over them
But you can rebuild them
That is even better
Do not run past every accomplishment to the next one
Make sure you live in the moment
Stop comparing yourself
It is not worth it
Stop dwelling on your past
You're wasting time being angry
Wasting years
Months
Days
Hours
Minutes
And Seconds
Wasting it on being angry
I promise that you can do better
If you want to waste your time
At least let it be on something that makes you happy

We Are All
POETRY